Portraits of Life

By

Mark Crouch

ISBN: 1-4033-8173-9 (ebook)
ISBN: 1-4033-8174-7 (Paperback)
ISBN: 1-4033-8175-5 (Dustjacket)

This book is printed on acid free paper.

1stBooks - rev. 10/23/02

Acknowledgements

I would like to dedicate this book to my parents, Philip and Hazel Crouch. Without them I would have none of the memories contained in this book. And especially to my mother for her endless hours of typing and offering her vast knowledge of the English language to try to help me. It went against her grain to type some blatant grammatical errors, but she did it anyway. Thank You both for all you mean to me.

Your Son, Mark Crouch

I would like to give special thanks to Mr. Jerry Barnett for his unique artistic contribution to this book.

I also would like to thank Mr. Kenneth Harl Jr. for helping me over the computer hurdles that were so high for me but so low for him.

And I would like to thank my family, my wife Ginger, my daughter Jessica, and my son Jamison, for allowing me the time and space to be alone long enough to write all these little rhymes.

And special thanks to God for giving me the gift of life, His Son, and the ability to think and write in rhyme.

Contents

Foreward

As long as there has been language there has been poetic expression. Without poetry where would we find literary beauty? Think for a moment: Without poetry there would be no Davidic Psalms, no thundering by the prophets, no Koran that expresses itself from thousands of minarets around the world, no Iliad or Odyssey, no hymns for the church. And on and on we could go.

In Portraits of Life there is added to this vast sweep of poetic literature the feelings of a young poet as he presents his journeys and observations. And what a wealth it is of vignettes of life, of the animal world, and of nature in its wide diversity. Memories of his past, such as,"Climbing the Mulberry Tree", will undoubtedly quicken like memories in those who read this unusual volume, and who explore with him experiences of everyday life. They should certainly have no difficulty identifying with him.

And in his somber moments he takes you on his poetical journey into life's unanswered questions and man's reason for being on this earth.

Enjoy its wide breadth of subject matter, as well as the poet's versatility in his use of rhythm and cadence.

Robert L. Silvers
Executive Publisher/Religion Editor
The Saturday Evening Post

A Day Like This

The sky so blue
The trees so green
The air so crisp
All washed and clean.
That's why I'm out
And dare not miss
To just soak up
A day like this.

When seasons change
I know they must
And all the trees
Turn shades of rust,
The air so thick
With morning mist
So splendid is
A day like this.

The acorns fall
And walnuts too.
The fields consumed
By heavy dew,
Who can explain
Such wondrous bliss
That happens on
A day like this?

The sunlight through
The forest green
Which gives all life
A different sheen.
It is as though
It seems to kiss
The whole earth on
A day like this.

Mark Crouch

Dogs

If dogs could talk, what would they say?
What secrets they've been told.
We'd probably blush to hear them
As our stories they unfold.

Why is it we're so honest
With our silly canine friends?
We'll even shed a tear
As though they truly understand.

There's something in their eyes we see
That causes us to melt.
That love we see or feel, it seems
Most everyone has felt.

If dogs could only speak to us
That'd probably ruin our fun.
For then they'd tell us what they think
About the yarns we've spun.

I guess we'll have to be content
To listen to them bark,
And try to figure out just why
They're happy as a lark.

I think I've learned the most from dogs
'Bout simple things in life,
And how a little walk can chase away
All stress and strife.

And dogs are good at listening
To what I've got to say,
And maybe if I'd be like them
Well, that's a better way.

It's true I love all kinds of dogs
In every shape and size.
And I thank God He put them here
To be part of our lives.

The Spring Called Ritter Mill

Though thirty-seven years have passed,
And through the years the miles amassed.
My travels bring me once again
Back to this place where I began.

My boyhood playground in the woods
That time forgot, so glad it could,
Is much the same as it was then,
It's nice to be back here again.

The spring still flows out from the rocks,
Where I would quickly shed my socks.
But now content to watch it flow,
And wondering where it might go.

There're beavers living out here now,
And they've been left alone somehow
To frolic in my playground here.
And build their home year after year.

It almost is as though I see
A little guy down there. That's me.
I wonder what my thoughts were then,
When I played here, I was ten.

I can't sit on the dam and wish
While gazing down to watch the fish.
For it's collapsed and broken down,
And seems to form a rocky frown.

So here I've come on my birthday,
And I hope to return someday.
I love this place and always will,
This lovely spring called Ritter Mill.

Thoughts Unknown

I wonder if I'll always have
The nagging thought that comes around,
Each time I write a poem down,
Is this the last one to be found?

What is a poem anyway?
Perhaps a thought just floating there,
That seems to form as from thin air,
And does its best my soul to bare.

Though I might search the universe
For lofty thoughts that I might find,
And try my best to round them bind,
The loosened chords inside my mind.

Alas, I'm just a simple man.
No lofty thoughts in me reside.
Or if they do, they seem to hide.
While searching, though, I love the ride.

Though I might try to calculate
How best this poem now to end,
I see no path around the bend
On which to you my message send.

Rockin' in My Chair

Tonight the Locust's melody I hear,
Is mighty appetizin' to the ear,
While I enjoy their sound through sultry air,
A-sittin' in my favorite rockin' chair.

The chorus that they sing this August eve',
Seems mine alone, their gift that I receive,
While I release my burdens and my cares,
A-sittin' in my favorite rockin' chair.

The sun all tucked away and put to bed,
And soon I too will lay my weary head,
But for a moment to the sky I stare,
A-sittin' in my favorite rockin' chair.

The fireflies, with lanterns turned up bright,
While Locusts serenade, is quite a sight,
I'm frozen to my seat, I will not dare,
Disturb them, from my favorite rockin' chair.

The crickets join this raucous chorus line,
Tonight's performance was just mighty fine,
And I've enjoyed the symphony they've shared,
While sittin' in my favorite rockin' chair.

If I Knew What Poets Think

What would James Whitcomb Riley think
About our world today?
Would he sit and write his poems
By a fake fireplace?

Would he own a cell phone
Or perhaps a Fax machine?
Maybe rather than a walk
He'd scooter down the lane.

I wonder if he'd surf the Web
Instead of read a book,
While waiting for his supper
In the microwave to cook.

And what would Mr. Riley think
About our President,
And how he stayed in office
Even after impeachment.

What would James Whitcomb Riley think
About the internet?
And could we find his poems
On the Web at James.net?

I really kind – a wonder
What he'd think of our fast pace.
Or if he'd sit there on his porch
And watch us like a race.?

Somehow I can't imagine him
All curled up on his bed.
To read his favorite E-book
Before laying down his head.

Some things are hard to picture
And to me this here is one.
To watch James Whitcomb Riley
At his laptop having fun.

Well, I'm content just knowing
That I'm doing what he did.
With pen in hand, on paper
Go ideas from my head.

The Lonesome Home

Tucked away and covered by
The forest's lovely dome,
There it's waiting patiently
The little lonesome home.

Vacant now for years
To watch the sunset all alone,
Beneath the canopy of spruce
This little lonesome home.

Why is it now abandoned
And left standing through these years?
At times when I drive by at sunset
I can feel its tears.

The forest has evaporated
'Round it all about.
And though it's deathly quiet here
I seem to hear it shout.

My family once so happy here,
Where do they now all roam?
That seems to be the cry I hear
From this sad, lonesome home.

The Cool Of Day

As I was in my garden
In the early morning light
Before the sun had crept its way up high,
The quiet stillness I enjoyed
Brought peaceful, pure delight,
As dreamily I gazed up to the sky.

As steam was gently rolling
O'er the surface of the lake,
No breath of wind disturbed its gentle flow.
I watched this wondrous earth
As it began to slowly wake,
And felt something God wanted me to know.

That this was still His favorite time
The coolness of the day,
When in His garden He would take a walk
With that first man and woman
And to them He'd gently say,
"Come with me so together we can talk."

But one day when they heard His sound
And knew it was the Lord,
They tried to hide themselves among the trees.
From that day entrance to the garden,
Blocked by flaming sword,
Would bring all of mankind then to their knees.

But on this morning as I walk
Here in the cool of day,
In this, my little garden, all alone,
It is as though I almost
Heard the Lord God gently say,
"I sent my Son for your sins to atone."

So as this day gets hot and steamy
While the sun climbs high,
There's something, Lord, that I would like to say,
"I'm thankful that we once again
Can to You now draw nigh,
And walk together in the cool of the day."

Grandma's Apple Roll

As memories often can distort,
Don't try to now console.
For mine are clear pertaining to
My Grandma's apple roll.

She'd bring it with her Sunday
For our lunch time after church.
But all the time we waited,
And then to it we would lurch.

It seems as though her recipe
Has fallen through the cracks.
Just thinking of it now
I feel my lips begin to smack.

When it was warm and real ice cream
Was layered on the top,
The taste would overwhelm you
Till you felt your head would pop.

You might think I'm exaggerating,
But I swear I'm not,
We all love Grandma's apple roll
Our whole consuming lot.

So as I sit here dreaming
With an empty china bowl,
My dreaming turns to rapture
Eating Grandma's apple roll.

Legs

Have I told you lately, Lord
I'm thankful for my legs?
That I'm not hopping 'round
Like pirates do on wooden pegs?

And I don't take for granted
How they carry me along
Through forests as I listen to the wind
And birds in song?

How many miles I wonder
Have these faithful legs of mine
Propelled me down the paths of life
Through fields of vast sunshine?

How legs are put together
Only You alone can know.
And what a mystery they are
Who knows what makes them go?

So as I walk I'm thankful, Lord
For legs that carry me.
And help me never to forget
To give my thanks to Thee.

This Little Poem

This little poem's short and sweet
Because I want to keep it neat.
Just so that it will fit the space
So all the words will take their place.

So all the words will take their place,
Just so that it will fit the space,
Because I want to keep it neat,
This little poem's short and sweet.

Just so that it will fit the space
'So all the words will take their place,
Because I want to keep it neat,
This little poem's short and sweet.

Because I want to keep it neat,
This little poem's short and sweet,
So all the words will take their place,
Just so that it will fit the space.

So all the words will take their place,
Just so that it will fit the space,
This little poem's short and sweet,
Because I want to keep it neat.

I could go on and on with this
But here I think that I must stop.
For if I don't I feel that soon
My eyes and head will simply pop.

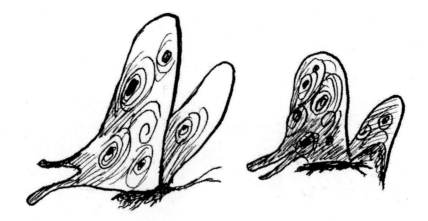

The Butterfly

He flew this way, then that way,
As if he didn't know,
Which way would be the right way
For this butterfly to go.

He acts as if he's just not sure
Of where he is at all,
And sometimes while he's in mid-flight
He'll go into a stall.

He'll seem to kinda' dawdle round
As if he's lost his way,
But then he just shoots off so fast
He'll take your breath away.

It's then I see what caught his eye,
What all this is about,
A female that he's chasing's
Making him just fly flat out.

No flying this way and then that,
But now just in straight lines.
And at such speeds you'd swear he's worried
He'll run out of time.

I never knew that butterflies
Could fly this fast, you see,
I just can't help but be amazed
And wish that it was me.

I'd no idea that butterflies,
Could reach that kind of speed.
I 'spose I'd never seen one
Who had just the proper need.

So off they flew and I was kinda' sad
To watch them go,
But from now on I'll never think
Of butterflies as slow.

Beyond The Blue

He peered directly at me
With penetrating eyes.
But then I noticed that he gazed
Not at me, but the sky.

Though seemingly unhurt
He lay there still, as dark of night,
A proud look on his face
And not the slightest glimpse of fright.

No doubt struck down by passing cars,
I'm sure by accident.
This stately Hawk that's lying here
Forever now silent.

I look once more, intently,
In his eyes that look so clear.
And cannot see a single shred
Of evidence there's fear.

His eyes, completely fixed
Upon the sky, which was his home,
Although, beyond the blue,
This Hawk will now forever roam.

This Old House

The old house with its shady lawn,
That brings to mind a time by-gone,
Would wave at travelers passing on,
Or greet them if they came at dawn.

The porch swing idle now it seems,
While round it this old house just gleams
And passers-by glance up and beam,
To see it now all washed and clean.

The Keswick Manor is its name,
And now I'd say its claim to fame.
The busy life, it tries to tame,
Outside its walls where nothing's sane.

This old house stood the test of time,
For these few days I called it mine.
And now I feel just so inclined,
To make its home here in this rhyme.

Equal

God didn't make a few of us,
And someone else, the rest.
I 'spose he made us everyone,
And none He likes the best.

The Turnedarounder I Get

My home in the hills here in Indiana,
Near the town Martinsville, where I live,
Has the curviest roads that you ever did see,
And a map of them I wish you'd give.

Though I love seeing what's just around the next curve,
Thinking I'll recognize it and yet,
The further I go, and the more that I see,
Is the turnedarounder I get.

To those of you who grew up driving these hills,
Now their mysteries I wish you would let
All their secrets come out,'cause when I drive these hills,
It's the turnedarounder I get.

So, won't you, oh, please, send that map to me now,
If you will, then I gladly will bet,
That no further I'll go down a road I don't know
And the turnedarounder I'll get..

Day to Day

Everything remains the same
From day to day.
Birds fly 'round and cows return
To eat their hay.

Horses, standin 'round in pastures
Knees bent while they rest.
Peacocks strutin 'round the barnyard
In their Sunday best.

Dogs begin their daylong barking
At the air it seems.
Cats just sit and watch them
While caught up in feline dreams.

As the sun begins to climb
High up in the sky,
All the fish out in the pond
Begin their daily dives.

Squirrels once again begin their play
Amongst the trees,
While overhead an eagle soars
And climbs a summer breeze.

Crows all gather for their daily meeting
So it seems,
While bluejays all upset by this
Just fly around and scream.

Amidst this noise a deer
Seems in a tranquil sort of mood,
And goes about her daily business·
Foraging for food.

'Coons and possums start their day
By climbing into bed,
Providing they can find a place
To rest their weary heads.

It's funny how the animals
Have no need to change,
They just accept their lot in life
And live, from day to day.

The Life One Might Have Lived

You ever wonder 'bout the life
You might have lived had you turned right?
But on the day that you turned left
That path you trod with all your might.

Not stopping then to wonder how
The road ahead might choose to bend,
Or contemplating all the while
The hearts that one might have to mend.

How can one glance upon years hence
The life that one has yet to live?
And judge astutely contributions
That one's life has yet to give?

Some say the road less traveled
Is the road one should embark upon.
But who's to say that travel there
Will guide one to the light of dawn?

Though some might wonder what's the use
To ponder on what might have been?
And run the risk of sinking deeply
Into thoughts to one's chagrin.

On further contemplation 'bout this life
That one just might have lived,
I find it much more satisfying
Thinking what I've yet to give

To those that in this life I live,
And down this path that I now tread,
I might be some encouragement
To their lives and what lies ahead.

The Lake

Each morning as I start my day
And gaze upon the lake,
It is as though it lies in wait
My dreams from me to take.

Then like a leaf that's gently blown
By early morning air,
It takes my dreams and guides them
Round the peaceful waters there.

Though often it's unnoticed
By so many who live round,
To me it's like a jewel
That has recently been found.

So now just like a friend who's there
To greet me when I wake,
It's ready then to dream with me
As each new dream I make.

Mom & Dad

No matter how much time goes by,
I feel the same when I draw nigh,
There's no time now for feeling sad,
'Cause I'm back home with Mom and Dad.

Though many miles between us now,
Back home it's just the same somehow,
To see them always makes me glad,
And be back home with Mom and Dad.

Too soon our time together gone,
And I will have to travel on,
But life's that way. I'll not be mad.
Just relish time with Mom and Dad.

My Friend Jack

I lost a Friend today,
And though we had moved far away,
We'd see each other now and then,
To sit and chat and laugh again,
For Jack, He was my Friend.

The stories he could share
I think He'd been most everywhere,
Around the world and back again,
While serving all his fellow men,
Oh Jack, He was my Friend.

And what quick wit he had,
Though some might think that he was mad,
You'd see the twinkle in His eye,
His wry ol' smile that could not lie,
For Jack, He was my Friend.

No time to say goodbye,
For I thought time was on our side,
That I'd be back to sit and chat,
And catch up on where life was at,
Oh, Jack, you were my Friend.

I don't know how to close,
And I don't want to, goodness knows,
But thanks to God, through faith in Him,
In heaven we'll meet up again,
For Jack, you are my Friend.

Sunday Afternoon Bliss

There's something quite peaceful I noticed one day,
How streets in the city grow calm on Sunday.

With cute little houses lined up in a row,
And the sun in its brilliance just bathing them so.

The streets and the yards are all looking so neat,
I mustn't be far from famed Lockerbie Street.

No traffic is snarling, no horns to be heard,
No voices are shouting, not even a word.

As leaves gently fall in the late autumn breeze,
I'd like, in my mind, for this moment to freeze.

My wish is each day would be peaceful like this,
And the whole world be like Sunday afternoon bliss.

The Old Gas Station

The ceiling's all caved in
Upon the place on which I sat.
Awaiting the next customer
We'd sit around and chat.

I'd run outside and pump their gas
And maybe check their oil.
Then fill their cooler full of ice
So all their food won't spoil.

The old gas station with the sign out front
That made 'em stop
To look at baby rattlers
While they stood and drank their pop.

I'd sweep the floors and stock the shelves,
But mainly sit around,
And talk about the olden days
When good times did abound.

I wonder where you'd go these days
To get your windshield cleaned?
The way that I could shine them up
They'd leave there with a gleam.

I'm sad to see the old gas station
Lying in a heap.
I'm sure if my old boss could see it
He'd just sit and weep.

Well, times have changed
And I'm still pumping gas most every day.
But now it's done by everyone.
Just not the same old way.

Crow Thoughts

The poor crow takes a beating
All day long
From all the little birds
This vicious throng.

The bluejay, quite relentless
In attack
Just simply won't get off
This poor crow's back.

I'm sure that he might wonder
What he's done,
When all he's after really
Is some fun.

And what's all this he hears
'Bout eating crow?
I'm sure that he just simply
Wants to know.

Just why he's ended up
With this bad rap?
From crows' perspective
It's a bunch of crap.

Father's Day

There really isn't time I'm 'fraid
To come up with a rhyme
For Father's day has seemed
To just slip up on me this time.

However, I just simply do not
Want to let the day
Just come and go and not take time
To stop and simply say

I'm just so happy you're my Dad
And always will be too,
Sometimes I feel so lucky
Like it's too good to be true.

So, in this short note
Let me take a moment just to say
"I love you, Dad,
And hope you have a Happy Father's Day."

Night Breeze

As I walk beneath the cliffs
And hear the brook just babbling there,
It seems as if there's nothing
Dare disturb the cool night air.

And as I climb the ridge
To glimpse the last rays of the sun,
It's hard to tell one's feelings
Knowing this day's almost done.

Did I accomplish anything
I set out for to do?
At daybreak all the plans I had
Now no time left to do.

As night time settles in
Upon the forest cool and green,
The birds begin to say good night,
Or 'least that's how it seems.

Their calls seem somewhat softer now
Like bedtime lullabies,
It seems the deer that crossed my path
Just now, seeks where to lie.

A fox just came into my view
A rare sight to behold,
His fur just seemed to shimmer
As I glimpsed the red and gold.

It's times like these I wish my bed
Were here among the trees,
And I could slowly drift to sleep
Caressed by the night breeze.

The Thing Below

When fallerin' the crick one day
A-huntin' rocks the same ole' way,
A'fore I knowd which way to go
The crick had up and gone below.

So walkin' in this dry crick bed
A-wonerin' why this crick's now dead.
An thinkin' that the spooky part
Is why this crick would now depart.

As I peered down into the hole
Where I had seen the water go,
I heard a funny sound behind,
Was somethin' there or just my mind?

As I looked 'round me everywhere,
And, like a deer, I sniffed the air.
And wonderin' what I might meet
I felt a tug down at my feet.

As I commenced to scream and then
I ran and not looked back again.
I'll bet you that I'll never go
Back to that place where down below,
There's things that took the crick down there
They're waitin' for me now, I'll swear.

So, if you're ever huntin' rocks
And see the crick begin to drop,
You'd best beware, or you might meet
That thing that grabbed me by my feet.

February Bliss

Oh day, your beauty overwhelms me.
Crystal is your sky.
Words could never paint this picture.
I can only sigh.

I have never seen a bluer blue,
Or greener green.
On this day even dead brown leaves
Give off a satin sheen.

The stream just seems to sparkle
As it slowly snakes its way
Around this mighty forest
On this most outstanding day.

It seems all wrong this time of year
To have a day like this.
But I for one will just have fun
In February bliss.

Country Life Sublime

There comes a time sometimes in life
When nothin' don't seem fun.
It's then that everywhere I look,
There's work that ain't got done.

Like all those stinkin dishes
Piled so high up in the sink,
The sight of which is 'bout enough
To send me o'er the brink.

And if that ain't enough
The kids commence to scream and shout.
And nothin I can say will stop 'em
As they tear about.

It's 'bout that time I run outside
Before I start to scream.
It seems like my whole life's become
Some sort of awful dream.

But then I heard the birds a-chirpin'
Glad-like in the trees,
And stopped to listen while I cooled down
In the summer breeze.

A dragon fly then caught my eye
Its body shinin' so,
Just sitin' on a flower out in the sun
Wings movin slow.

I saw a chipmunk sprawled out
On a big ole' pile o'junk.
The way his legs were danglin off it
Looked as though he's drunk.

Seemed everything outside my house
Was peaceful-like and calm.
While inside everything looked like
We'd been hit by a bomb.

It's then that I decided
Things around here's got to change.
We least could live as peaceful
As the cows out on the range.

If they're so dumb then why are they
So peaceful all the time?
I think our place could use
A little dose of the sublime.

My Three Room School

The three room school that I attended
When I was a boy,
Has brought to mind my teacher
Whom I loved to just annoy.

His name was Floyd,
A name you just don't hear much anymore.
I'll bet you, though, my presence
He could not seem to ignore.

'Twas bad enough
To spend the fifth and sixth grade in one room.
But what his life was like in those days,
I can but assume.

I still can smell the crayons
On the radiator there.
The smell they made while melting slowly,
Wafting through the air.

I'm sure he taught us something,
But I can't remember now.
Except for that old milk machine,
Its spout just like a cow.

I can't remember now
If I made good grades or all bad.
I hope this memory
Doesn't make my mother kind of sad.

Now, like so many things
The three room schools are mostly gone.
But in my mind the memory of that school
Lives on and on.

In looking back I really have fond memories
Of that time,
And Floyd, your three room school
Has found its home here in this rhyme.

Your Wedding Day

I've known this day would come,
I'd see my little girl,
Go gliding down the aisle,
All gone, her baby curls.

Though wedding bells now ring,
And joyful is the show,
Just spare a moment now,
There's something you must know.

It's hard for me to say,
The way I feel right now,
To tell you of my love,
I'll try real hard somehow.

No words can come to mind,
Mere thoughts cannot express,
My love for you today,
Donned in your wedding dress.

Your striking beauty pales,
To how I feel inside,
Forever will my love,
Of you closely abide.

Simpleminded Nimblewits

Simpleminded Nmblewits.
Seems everywhere there's idiots,
Who love to tear down those they meet,
And laugh at those knocked off their feet.

The kind of people they've become
Might make you think their mind's gone numb,
The only thing that brings them joy,
Is really nothing but a ploy.

On helping out, "Oh, yes", they would,
If only it makes them look good.
Don't be misled by folks like these,
They'd gladly bring you to your knees.

Yes, Simpleminded Nimblewits
The world abounds with idiots
Make no mistake, though, one thing's sure
That for this type there is no cure.

Winds Of Change

I've heard March comes in a-roarin'
But on this November day,
Through the air all things are soarin'
Blowin' us away.

If there're any leaves left hangin'
After this day's gone,
More than likely they're just stubborn
And like hangin' on.

Like them I don't want to give in
And let go of fall.
Out of all the seasons
It's the prettiest of all.

But I've no doubt that wind like this
Is blowin' in a change,
If your home's not tied down today
You'll be blown off the range.

So on this first day of November
What a sight to see,
Like everything is sideways
As the wind howls through the trees.

I hope it's just a fluke
And not a sign of things to come,
Or this might be a long cold winter
'Fore it's said and done.

51

The Most Forgotten Bird

Of all the birds that come to feed
In my backyard today,
There's one I always overlook
Amidst the bird array.

The Junco, and the Titmouse,
And the Bluejays all are there,
The Chickadee is also munching
On the mixed bird fare.`

There're three kinds of woodpeckers
That come around to eat,
While on the ground the Eastern Towhee's
Shuffling his feet.

Brown headed Cowbirds crowd around
To see they get their share,
While sounding like a dripping faucet
Heads high in the air.

Indigo Buntings on a branch
Are rare to see indeed,
Yet this one can't resist the urge
To come and eat my seed.

The Thrush stays on the ground
To get what others leave behind,
While joined there by the Mourning Dove
So peaceful and sublime.

An Eastern Bluebird comes around
Not often, though, you see
As does the common Grackle
Who's all purple and shiny.

I love to watch the Nuthatch
Who defies all gravity,
The way he walks up trees that way
Is quite a sight to see.

And then there is the Hummingbird
The fastest of them all,
But when he stops to rest
I'm just amazed that he's so small.

The Cardinal and Goldfinch
Are the prettiest I see,
Their red and yellow seems to glow
In contrast to the trees.

The Housefinch with his red head
Comes around most everyday,
And all the while the little Wren
Just flits around in play.

The Robin isn't drawn at all
To this activity,
She seems content to munch on worms
Observing passively.

I've even had wild turkeys come
Along with Hawks and Crows,
Sometimes the seed won't last the day
But that's just how it goes.

Of course the ever present Squirrel
And Chipmunks stuff their face,
While late at night Raccoons come out
And tidy up the place.

Of all the birds that come here
The most common one of all,
Is the one God says that He takes note of
When it falls.

Yes, it's the tiny Sparrow
That God says He watches o'er,
But He said that to let us know
He loves us even more.

So when you see a Sparrow
Be reminded of God's care,
No matter where you are
You can be sure God sees you there.

Ants

There're times I wish I were an ant
Not questioning the why,
But simply going 'bout my work
Until the day I die.

Not taking time to bother
With complaining 'bout my lot,
That I've been given in this life
And liking it or not.

When obstacles present themselves
The ants find ways around,
And when they do it's then they find
That freedom does abound.

I stand and watch and wonder
What it is that drives them so?
These ants are constant motion
Never moving very slow.

They seem to work together
Just as though some common goal
Propels them on to do their work;
There's something I must know.

How can I take what I've observed
And to my life apply?
Some simple truth to help me live
A much more fruitful life?

Just maybe persevere
Is what the ants would like to say,
And they've all done their best to teach me
In their own small way.

Ghost Trees

It held them fast

Locked in its grasp.

These ghost-like trees

With withered knees.

Their fingers ripped

'Neath winter's grip.

Their twisted forms

Morose, forlorn.

Left all alone

To writhe and moan

In landscape white

With ghostly fright.

Yet they abstain

From winter's pain.

Now fast asleep

As winter creeps.

Await spring breeze

These ghost-like trees.

Mark Crouch

The Old Crawdad

He walks around the little creek
While sideways he does go,
When something kind'a scares him
He backs up real fast, you know.

His pinchers ever probing
Under leaves, for food I guess.
But then as if he pinched himself
He stirs up quite a mess.

He meanders kind'a lazy like
As if he's got all day.
And then he just shoots off so fast
You're not quite sure which way.

And then I spot the old crawdad
A way on down the creek.
It's then I see he's finally found
Himself something to eat.

My Backyard

When I'm in my backyard,
The world seems oh so far away.
To watch the moon rise slowly,
As it says good-bye to day.

The chaos that I hear about
Throughout the world tonight
Seems far removed from here
I feel no terror and no fright.

In spite of all the stars
That seem to twinkle in the sky,
I know that war is raging,
And tonight, that some will die.

I wish the whole wide world
Could come and sit in my backyard,
For here there's no destruction,
Not the slightest little shard.

I'm thankful that for now
My backyard's quiet and serene,
From here I pray for just one day
When folks won't be so mean.

Laguna

As I sit back and lazily
Let my thoughts drift by,
It's memories of a beach town
That I see in my mind's eye.

Laguna Beach, in California
Is my favorite one,
No finer place that I have been
To watch the setting sun.

The silhouette of Catalina
As the sun goes down,
And waves are crashing on the rocks
While pelicans glide 'round.

Has got to be a sight
That I will never tire to see,
Though I'm in Indiana now
It's crystal clear to me.

I love to wander through the tide pools,
Creatures to behold,
The wonders that they hide there
Mystify the young and old.

The palm trees clinging to the cliffs
Defy all gravity
As though they're trying desperately
From falling to the sea.

The flowers and the trees
That mingle delicately here
Create an artist's paradise
That lasts throughout the year.

The morning fog that has a sweet aroma
All its own,
Is seasoned lightly with the sea's
Own salty, thick sea foam.

I've really never left the sea
There in Laguna Beach.
Its memories often flood my mind
And those I now beseech.

The Pond

It lay in a peaceful slumber
While the world around it quaked.
Oblivious to all the world outside
And here, no wake.
For this pond sleeps in a dreamy haze
Not mindful of the passing days.

Not even mighty winds that blow
Can stir this little place.
For slumber's written deeply
In the wrinkles of its face.
So safely tucked within its cage,
This little pond while nations rage.

Why can't we then like it exist
In a peaceful harmony?
Like beavers, ducks and all these birds
In close proximity?
I guess that's just too much to ask,
For humans, a most daunting task.

Unlike the creatures who live here
In their world all tucked away,
We just can't seem to co-exist
Just live from day to day.
I think it grieves the heart of God
Who made this earth for all who trod.

When Squirrels Fly

Ever seen a flying squirrel?
I saw one fly today.
At first I thought it was a leaf
Just floating down my way.

But then it came so fast at me
It took my breath away,
And then it landed on a tree
Just a few feet away.

I got a real good look at him
But then he glanced my way.
And just as fast as he had come
I watched him glide away.

My hope is forty years won't pass
Until I see the day,
Another flying squirrel decides
To glide on down my way.

Seasons

There's a cold wind blowing
Through our little town today.
I'm sure it won't be long now
Before winter comes our way.

To me there's something kind of sad
About this time of year,
To see the leaves upon the ground
All dead and withered there.

It hurts a little knowing
That the garden stopped its growing,
That there won't be any peppers
Left to pickle, or to pick.

And as I watch the steam
That's slowly rising off the lake,
As though the cold is sneaking in
Its warmth from it to take.

To hear the guns up in the hills
Round here's just part of life,
But I don't like to think about
Deer running for their life.

And though the sun is out today
I cannot feel its heat.
The warmth has seemed to vanish
In the air that smells so sweet.

There're very few things left
That show the signs of summer's green.
And soon the forest floor
Will shimmer white with winter's sheen.

But soon I'll wake one morning
To a crystal morning glee.
And marvel at the beauty
Of the ice that coats the trees.

'Tis then sad feelings fade away
Of summer, come and gone.
And just like a new day
Another season has begun.

I know now that I shouldn't be
So sad when leaves do fall.
But just enjoy each season
And the wonder of it all.

The Rubble Of Our Lives

This day will always be remembered
For the tragedy,
And shows us once again the dregs
Of man's depravity.

The loss of life today
Here in the good old USA
Is far too much to comprehend
On such a gorgeous day.

The sun was shining brightly
As we all began to reel
From hearing news that left us
Not quite knowing how to feel.

They're calling this an act of war
But those who lost their lives
Weren't wearing any uniforms
While at them planes did dive.

A senseless act is what they say,
But isn't war like that?
They'll hunt the one responsible
And kill him like a rat.

And though I have no doubt
That it will happen as they say,
There's nothing that will change the outcome
Of this dreadful day.

So as we pray for those
Who lost their loved ones on this day.
I also pray that God would show us
How to walk His way.

For when our life is over
Just one thing will matter then,
That Christ was found there in our hearts
Then new life will begin.

Written September 11, 2001

Dreaming

I used to dream when I was young
Of places that I'd go, far flung,
Around this great big world of ours,
Oh how I'd dream, for hours and hours.

Across the seas I'd sail, and then,
Through storms and all the fiercest winds
I'd sail back to this land of ours,
Oh, how I'd dream, for hours and hours.

Like great explorers I would go
Through forests in the blinding snow,
To blaze a trail I'd trudge for hours,
Oh how I'd dream, for hours and hours.

While running through the fields 'round home
Across the pastures I would roam,
Then caught by spring's warm summer showers,
Oh how I'd dream, for hours and hours.

Now time's gone by and boyhood's gone,
But dreams, they just keep rollin' on,
And if time won't cause me to sour,
I still can dream, for hours and hours.

The Verse

Lately I have heard it said
That poems in the verse are dead.
Their widespread popularity
Now gone with their hilarity.

But may I, though one voice, be heard,
And utter now a spoken word?
And with it a most loud lament
For verses that are heaven sent?

I find no solace in the prose,
Though try I might, oh goodness knows.
They sound to me, most times perverse,
And leave me longing for the verse.

My hope is that I won't offend,
For that would bring me to an end!
Your feelings of me then quite terse
When all I've done is speak in verse.

So let me now just quickly close,
Though I just can't do that in prose,
For if I could, I would rehearse
But all that comes to mind is verse!

Remember When

When I was just a boy
Life seemed so simple then,
My peanut butter sandwich
Eaten 'neath my roof of tin.
My baseball bat, my ball, and glove
Were always close at hand.
It seems my life was simple
As I just remember when.

When I was just a boy
I always loved the sun,
When I awoke and saw it out
Adventure had begun.
Just romping out across the fields
To me, was plenty fun.
Oh, how my life was simple
As I played there in the sun.

When I was just a boy
I never planned ahead.
I didn't understand the feelings
I know now of dread.
I never gave a thought
To what in that day lay ahead,
I just enjoyed what crossed my path
Till I fell into bed.

When I was just a boy
Out sleeping 'neath the stars,
It seemed like I was far away
Yet not so very far.
My parents never put me down
Or my young dreams did mar,
For ours was just a simple life
And me, their little star.

When I was just a boy
I led a simple life.
I had no time for worry
And I knew not much of strife.
But see, I'm still that little boy
Deep down inside my life.
The thought of losing simple things
Just cuts me like a knife.

When I was just a boy
Life seemed so simple then.
I never gave much thought
To growing up to be a man.
But now that I'm much older
And here writing with my pen,
I love to think of simple things
As I remember when.

The Swan's Song

Beguiling beauty, charming grace,
Wondrous façade that hides my face.
Look deep within my eyes, you'll see
An evil lurks inside of me.

I'm more like you than you might know.
Just look beyond this mask of snow.
Enchanting, as you watch me glide,
Don't turn your back while by my side.

The song I sing is graceful, true,
Come closer now I beg of you.
Oh let me sing my song once more,
Its rapturous tune you will adore.

My name is Swan, and 'round me see,
A peaceful, haunting melody.
Yet my song's like a viper's tune,
Might I bite you here 'neath the moon?

Turning Forty

I just can't think of anything
That's funny 'bout this day,
For what could be so funny
When your hair starts turning gray?

I've heard it said when forty hits
It's all downhill from there,
So now you'll know the reason
When you start to lose your hair.

But please don't let it bother you
When people like to say,
That turning forty's really just
Another average day.

'Cause deep inside you'll know
They're either crazy, or a nut,
So try to just avoid the urge
To kick them in the butt.

I hope that I've encouraged you
To just enjoy the day,
And not believe those things 'bout forty
People always say.

Dedicated to Scott

The Mockingbird

Mornings wouldn't be the same
Without the Mockingbird.
For he makes up for all the rest
That utter ne'er a word.

I really don't believe he's learned his songs
From other birds.
For I think he's composing,
Even making up new words.

He's really quite amazing,
How he never seems to tire,
Of serenading all the world
While perched atop a briar.

Why is it I don't seem to recognize
The songs he sings?
But simply welcome gladly
All the tidings that he brings.

I guess I'd have to say
Of all the birds here in the world,
My favorite one is simply
The amazing Mockingbird.

The Perfect Place

There's no place that I'd rather be than here,
Beside this lovely creek so pure and clear.

Tucked far away out here deep in the woods,
I'd come here everyday if I just could.

Forget the big resorts and all the rest,
To me this place right here is simply best.

Some people search forever, not to find,
A place of vast contentment that's now mine.

Clocks ·

I don't know what time it is,
And I don't really care.
For I've begun to hate the clock
Its presence over there.

The ceaseless ticking loudly
On the mantle up above,
I've half a mind to go right now
And give the thing a shove.

Seems everywhere I look today
There sits another clock.
I think to be obsessed with time this way
Is just a crock.

I'd like to know who started this.
I wish they'd show their face
I hope they're happy for the way
They've changed the human race.

For now our world revolves around
The face of all these clocks.
Each day the first thing that I hear
Is just, 'tick tock, tick tock'.

No time for this. No time for that.
The clock says I must go.
Now hold on just a minute here,
There's something I must know.

Could just for once the world forget
The clocks up on the wall?
If just for one day, I'll bet that day
Life would be a ball.

The Meaning of Life

Did you ever try to think
Just what there is to Life?
Well, if you need an answer to
That question, ask my wife.

'Cause she'll be glad to tell you
What this life is all about,
And if you don't know where to
Start, she'll help you work that out.

It's really pretty simple
If you've got the time to hear,
So sit down and don't interrupt,
And listen with both ears.

The answer to life's question
Became clear to her one day.
'Twas then our children
Came into the world as if to say,

"Your life is now about
The busy lives we are to lead,
And getting us to things on time
Is your priority."

So now you know just what this life
Is truly all about.
And if you don't agree with me
Sit down and do time out!

The Cabin

I had a special place to go
When as a boy I wandered so.
But not far did I have to roam
To this dear place so close to home.

This little cabin that I had
Was built with care by me and Dad.
With each board neatly laid in place,
A sense of pride soon graced my face.

From home a mere stone's throw away,
This little cabin quaintly lay.
But in my mind it seemed far flung
From all that I then lived among.

I had a stove where I burned wood,
And cooked my food as best I could.
While on cold nights I'd stoke the fire,
And from it warmth, all I desired.

But many mornings I would wake,
While in my bed I'd gently shake,
And watch my breath in billows form,
Big lazy clouds each frosty 'morn.

I'll not forget my lantern's light,
As shadows danced with all their might
Upon the ceiling from within
My little secret boyhood den.

Its walls were covered from outside
With rabbit fur and squirrel hide.
Like Daniel Boone I strove to be
Who was this that now lived in me?

As I think back upon times then
And wonder how life might have been
Without my little cabin there,
I think I'd feel a deep despair.

But fondly as I reminisce
About the cabin I now miss,
Its quiet comfort I recall,
That meant to me the most of all.

Passed On

And now the blue gray haze of summertime,
Settles like a blanket o'er the hills.
Just like steamy rain,
Tears pour down again.
Left all alone remembering you still.

Now like a missing puzzle piece that's lost,
I wonder why you went away at all?
Leaving me to grope,
Lost, and with no hope.
Your leaving has on my life cast a pall.

I've never known such loneliness before,
And how a heart can feel turned inside out.
Like a wave at sea,
Crashing endlessly.
You were what my life was all about.

But black of night must always then give way
Unto the light that comes with each new dawn.
Though I'm lonely now,
I'll get through somehow,
I won't forget you now that you've passed on.

Giants By The Sea

I'll not forget the day
I saw the giants by the sea.
And heard their mournful cry
As they were calling out to me.

"Come on in, my friend,"
It was as though I heard them say.
"It's quiet, calm, and peaceful here,
Just come on in our way."

I marveled at their size
While ever deeper I did go,
The stillness there squelched every sound
From crashing waves below.

The carpet that I walked upon
I knew was centuries old.
The sunlight seemed to transform ferns
From green, to shades of gold.

Though pounding of the sea
Can have a soothing, calming charm,
The peacefulness I felt in there would that,
Quickly disarm.

I must return one day
To see those giants by the sea,
Until then I will hear them
Gently calling out to me.

Wondrous Days

Just when I think my mind's gone blank
I've nothing left to say,
That's when this wondrous world of ours
Just takes my breath away.

A honey bee just working on a flower
Out in the sun,
Kinda' makes me wonder
If to him it's work or fun.

About the time I'm feeling hot
A breeze begins to blow,
And where it comes from I'm convinced
That only goodness knows.

And butterflies so paper thin
How do they get around?
Yet they can fly quite fast at times
Without so much a sound.

A hummingbird with wings so fast
You'd swear he'd none at all,
And when he stops to rest a spell
I can't believe how small.

I could go on forever
Citing our world's wondrous ways,
But I am sure I just don't have
Enough of wondrous days.

Fabrications

No sadder a sound could I think of tonight
Then the sound of good-bye
From a love taken flight
And the feeling I see in a teary-eyed glance
Spells the doom of our faded and jaded romance.

Was it ever a love that we truly did feel
In our hearts for each other
That seemed very real?
Or have we been good friends, unbeknown to us both?
All the while through this season
We're known as betrothed.

How can love come and go
And then truly depart
Like the skip of a beat from my now broken heart?
Is our love just like that, sometimes good, sometimes bad?
Such reality is what now leaves me so sad.

For no sadder a song could I sing you tonight
Then the song of good-bye from a love taken flight.
And its melody clear
Through a teary-eyed glance
Sings the doom of our jaded and faded romance.

This Thing Called Spring

It's Spring again!
All things are new.
The daffodils
Are popping through.
The busy birds
Are nesting too.
Earth's waking up
To life anew.

The lightning cracks
The thunder booms.
Not far behind
A storm there looms.
Then down it pours
Such heavy rain.
Spring's melody
Of glad refrain.

At night new growth
Can scant be heard
Push through the leaves,
Don't breathe a word.
I've never heard
This sound before.
Have I unlocked
Some secret door?

And oh, the birds,
Such boisterous song.
They all join in,
One happy throng
To welcome Spring
This joyful time.
And add their tune
To such a rhyme.

Words can't describe
A purple field.
Such glorious hue
At sunset yield.
Or how the clouds,
Like drapery hang
On this Spring night
When bullfrogs sang.

This thing called Spring,
I'll never know
How I might best
Describe it so.
In one word, Hope,
It gives to me.
This wondrous Spring-like
Melody.

Mark Crouch

The Midnight Sun

When once I traveled to a frozen land
Quite far away,
This weekend was the famous July fourth
And I had heard that here
Is where they have the longest day,
At midnight still the sunshine will pour forth

Of course this is Alaska
Some say it's the last frontier,
Where wild beasts still roam around and play.
I wanted more than anything
To on my first night here
See midnight sunshine glisten on the bay.

Seemed everywhere I looked
The stunning beauty of the place
Was overwhelming, too much to take in.
And when I still could feel the sun at midnight
On my face,
I found it hard to not just sit and grin.

Alaska, I was really here,
'Twas too hard to believe,
So far from my old Indiana home.
The beauty 'round each corner
I found too much to conceive,
But I continued gladly there to roam.

One day I stopped to take a closer look
At this large moose,
Who by the road was grazing peacefully.
But what I thought was solid ground
Turned into tundra juice,
And down I went quite quickly to my knees

The moose just kinda' glanced at me
Like I was some buffoon.
He'd probably seen such foolishness before.
But as I got up to my feet
And feeling like a goon,
I know now what their legs are longer for.

The next day I went fishing
Some say for the Halibut,
A little joke intended there you see.
But it's no joke
To get one of these guys into your net,
They fight to stay in their gray, murky sea.

I love the little Otters
Who lie floating on their back
As though they've not a care in life at all
Reclining as it were
On their own personal hammock.
Out here I too feel monumentally small.

So on the birthday of our country
Here in this vast land
In what is fondly called the Kenai Fjords,
I want to thank the Maker
Who created this by hand,
The one and only mighty sovereign Lord.

The Fox Who Ate the Peacock

There can, but only one, be ruler
Of a ranch so grand,
Its role has clearly been mine from the start.
For long before the stranger came to this,
My true homeland,
I've loved this place for years with all my heart.

This Texas ranch has been my family's home
For decades now,
We roamed its pastures as we kept close watch.
But on to it has strayed a peacock
Though I don't know how,
I 'spose he thinks this Fox's plans he'll botch.

He struts around as though he owns the place
With feathers spread,
As though all should take note and humbly bow.
But he is unaware
That there's a price now on his head,
The value though I'll not reveal right now.

He stays close by the ranch house
For his master to admire,
Enjoying admiration from them all.
Completely unaware
His life is sadly, strangely dire,
His every feather radiates his gall.

He moves about the ranch
Each step is unimpeded grace,
His feathery bouquet for all to see.
Though cunningly I plan a horror
To enshroud his face,
I must admit it's hard to squelch my glee.

The moment I've been waiting for
Has finally arrived,
As stupidly he strays away from home.
Then down the path he finally treads
Long which I've now connived,
And waited patiently for him to roam.

The poor fool never knew what hit him
When I made my charge,
As stealthily my teeth then found their mark.
Then I exulted in my prize
And such a prize so large,
That to consume it I must now embark.

I left a trail of plumage
As I dragged him to my den,
Where on this Peacock now my family dines.
Though some might view my actions
As the gravest of the sins,
To me this meal quite simply was divine.

Deep Things

Of all the deep thinkers that lived on this earth,
And all of the thoughts that they thought,
I wonder which one was the deepest of all,
Or has time simply up and forgot?

What is a deep thought might I ask of you now?
Oh please, a deep thinker reply.
Could you offer a glimpse of what's waiting beyond?
For one day I'm destined to die.

What were the deep things you discovered out there
When you spent those two years by the lake?
Could mankind somehow benefit from what you learned?
Well, if so, what's the difference it makes?

The Bible says no mind conceives of the plans
That God has for us waiting beyond.
If our thinking can't lead us to God
Then our time would be wasted out there by the pond.

My humble conclusion then points to a path
Where God's Spirit ahead of me trod.
And I simply now will just follow
If I'm to discover the deep things of God.

Real

"What is real?" I asked myself
At sunset one fine day,
For as I watched, its beauty
Slowly faded into gray.

Or like a bird so full of life
One moment, then it's gone,
Struck down, now lying in a ditch
No more to sing its song.

So what is real? Are things I see
And feel, really so?
Or just some grand illusion
That I'm not yet meant to know?

For just the word itself
Cannot be touched or felt or seen,
There're times I wake up thinking
What was real, was just a dream.

There's one thing that I found out
In my search for what is real,
Reality's not based upon
What I see, think, or feel.

So what is real? The dictionary
Says the meaning's true,
So must I now go on a quest
To find this meaning too?

The Word of God says Jesus
Is the Way, the Truth, the Life,
My search for what is real
Can end right here, in Jesus Christ.

Winging It

In early morning,
Misty fields lie silent in the dawn,
As on them longingly I calmly stare.
Would but this morning gladly live forever.
On and on,
And with me, all its beauty then to share.

How might I capture such a calm,
And in my mind implant,
To then retrieve when needed at my will?
When life and those within it,
Seem to blindly, loudly rant,
I'll now simply erase them with my quill.

Like A Child

Like a child I am to be.
Trusting, Lord, of Thee.
If I am to live with You
Through all eternity.

Make my eyes be once again
Like a child's, so true,
Gazing ever upward
And intently trusting you.

Help me, Lord, to now become
Like that child so fair,
While my hand slips into Thine
Lead me upward there.

As your sheep, my Shepherd be,
Guide me to my home.
I will follow trustingly
All of me now own.

"Well, Good"

When telling my tale to my neighbor,
The old farmer who lived next door,
I noticed a look that appeared on his face
Was I now becoming a bore?

He continued to smile through the yarn that I spun,
And just whittled away at his wood.
And when it appeared I had come to an end,
He just looked up and said, "Well, good".

But as I continued my story,
The old farmer just smiled and looked down.
Though watching him closely I never could tell
If I noticed a hint of a frown.

Though try as I might to engage him,
He just earnestly whittled his wood.
And then in response to my story I'd shared
He just grinned slightly and said, "Well, good".

The lesson I learned from him that day
I would like to now share if I could.
When someone tells you their whole story,
Just smile gently and say, "Well, good".

My Mulberry Tree

In my days of childhood
Lies a memory,
The time I spent in branches
Of my big Mulberry tree.

I can't remember now the taste
Of fresh mulberry pie.
But I can sure remember
Plucking fruit from branches high.

But fondest of the memories
Of that tree I now recall,
Is how I'd pick a slew of berries,
Then just eat them all.

No doubt I would emerge
With purple stain upon my face,
And probably on my clothes as well
While Mother beckoned grace.

I can't remember if I ever
Ate more than I should.
But if there'd been a limit to them,
Then I'm sure I would.

Yep', that's my favorite tree of all
That as a boy I'd climb.
And that's why I felt so inclined
To 'bout it write this rhyme.

One Afternoon in May

Soft breezes cause the wildflowers in full bloom
To gently sway.
As I observe creation
On one afternoon in May.

The geese with goslings close behind
Explore their placid lake,
As I along with them enjoy
One afternoon in May.

While listening to the woodpeckers
My thoughts quickly give way,
How blessed I am to be here
On this afternoon in May.

How to describe the fragrance
Of a field of new mown hay,
In one word it's delightful
On one afternoon in May

Beside this lake so peaceful
There's no need for nerves to fray,
As I soak up this atmosphere
One afternoon in May.

As sunlight glistens on the lake
I'm carried far away
From every troubling thought I have
This afternoon in May.

In fact I can't recall just one
This much to my dismay,
All problems solved right here it seems
One afternoon in May.

Spoutin Off

When life's aggravatin' and all you can do
Is manage to maintain your cool.
That's better than just given' in to the urge
To makin' yourself out a fool.

'Cause there's no doubt there're times
In this life that we live,
That you'd rather just quit and give up.
But that's when I find
The most comforting thing
Is to just tell myself to shut up.

Now I know I can always find someone out there
Who's a whole lot more worse off than me.
But somehow that's no consolation for times
When I'm driven' by life up a tree.

Now I will not give in to that stupid cliché
That when it rains it then will just pour.
And right here I have firmly implanted my foot
In the backside of all that folklore.

Front Porch Time

I think that everybody needs some front porch time.
To sit and rock and let the breezes blow your mind.

Down one path, then the other, without knowing where
It then will come to rest, and also, not to care.

To take the time to say "Hello" to passers-by,
It seems to be a lost art simply saying "Hi".

I hate to think for my kids that those times are gone,
Our lives today so furious as they press on.

Yes, people need more front porch time, or least I think,
Perhaps it'd save a few from going o'er the brink.

Some Hazy Morn

The haze that hovers oe'r the corn
In August on this sultry morn,
Is like a blanket to adorn
This field that once looked so forlorn.

And in the light given by the sun
On this day, though it's just begun,
I think of all the work not done
And wonder if there'll be time for fun.

I know that heat is on its way
And not so very far away.
It creeps its way right through the hay
As it encompasses this day.

So as the sun begins to blaze
And burn up all the morning haze,
I now can watch the cattle graze
On distant hills, 'pon which I gaze.

It's beauty only that I see
And that is what inspires me
While gazing out from 'neath this tree
Upon this field in shades of green.

And in the afternoon again
The haze returns to blanket then
The hills, the valleys, and the glen
I wonder if it's always been.

So now as evening settles o'er
This sultry, hazy, field of corn,
I'll hope to see a new day born
Some lovely, sultry, hazy morn.

My Dog Jiggs

My dog Jiggs was a wearisome sort.
He never could learn to fetch.
He would jump and then writhe and his body contort,
He was truly a miserable wretch.

He could not settle down and was never content
To allow me to pet him without
Jumping up in my face till my patience was spent,
All the while slobber poured from his snout.

Now Jiggs was a handsome dog, there was no doubt,
To his fur a magnificent sheen.
But if brains were an attribute he was without,
He's the dumbest dog I'd ever seen.

Now hard as it was for me then to accept,
I decided to give him away,
And my feelings about that till now have been kept
Bottled all up inside till today.

So my only thought now as I look back in time
To the day poor 'ole Jiggs did depart
Is how thankful I am to him now for this rhyme,
And its merriment brought to my heart.

Portraits Of Life

With each new day the Master would begin
His canvas blank.
What would the portrait be at this day's end?
Would He be happy with His work,
As slowly the sun sank?
Or would this portrait need His graceful mend?

Perhaps today the painting
Is an orphan on the street.
Some little boy or girl with cup in hand,
Where in any major city of the world,
This kind you'll meet.
The backdrop of this painting's not so grand.

How 'bout a family picnic
By a peaceful mountain lake?
The snow capped peaks behind them glistening,
With all their smiling faces,
What a portrait this would make.
This painting, one can almost hear birds sing.

But on this day the Master
Has to grimace at the scene,
As He begins to paint with trembling stroke.
For lying face down in a pool of blood
On streets so mean
A boy, while family in their tears then choke.

On this day with the canvas clean
In early morning dawn,
With dewdrops heavy and the air so sweet,
A mother deer goes gliding
Close behind her two twin fawn.
The ground just glistens underneath their feet.

Again with canvas clean
The Master spies a bumblebee.
From flower to flower it moves in search of food.
No doubt this portrait will be sweet
For every eye to see,
As it portrays a wondrous spring-like mood.

Then, sadly faced with yet
Another portrait of this life
That we here on this earth must daily live,
The Master, though reluctantly,
Portrays a family's strife.
With each stroke ponders what must finally give.

But, thankfully, the Master
Paints a rainbow in the sky
For all mankind to witness and behold,
And through it offer hope,
Though His own Son here had to die.
Through Him, the Master one day we'll behold.

Whispering Pines

The sound the wind makes as it rustles
Through the pine trees here,
Is whispering gentle melodies
Now softly to my ear.

The air is laden sweetly
With a fragrance that's unmatched.
And under foot the carpet of pine needles,
Neatly thatched.

The canopy above me
And the ferns so thick below,
I feel the urge to whisper
As I pass through here real slow.

The sunlight does its best
To penetrate these stately trees,
And moonlight through the pines is lovely
In the evening breeze.

So as I leave behind me now
This gorgeous grove of pine,
I'll plant the sound the wind makes here
Quite firmly in my mind.

Not Dreaming of White

Seems everyone is dreaming
Christmas will come in all white.
But then I'd have to shovel down the walk
With all my might.

I know it looks all pretty
Stuck to hills, and roads, and trees.
I'm sure my kids would love it
If it piled up to their knees.

But what if on the way to Grandma's house
On Christmas Day,
Our car slides off the road
In all that snow, along the way?

I wonder if we'd still be smiling
Or would there be frowns
While peering out the windows of our car
While upside down.?

I know it's pretty
When the treetops glisten with new snow.
The sight of which can bring to all our faces
Quite a glow.

But as the children listen
To the crunching metal sound,
The glistening snow up in the tree we hit
Comes pounding down.

So, if it's quite all right with you,
No Christmas cards I'll write.
'Cause I'm not dreaming
That this year our Christmas will be white.

The Passing Of The Buck

Majestic was the creature
That across my path did roam.
As I made my way unto
My little country home.

Just seeing him in all his glory,
I was then awe-struck,
For I was now a witness to
The passing of the Buck.

That saying so familiar to me
Had now changed its tune.
The night I saw him clearly
'Neath the light of the full moon.

The memory of him now forever
I will neatly tuck.
The night I was a witness to
The passing of the Buck.

That old familiar saying
Simply from my mind now suck.
For now I know true meaning to
The passing of the Buck.

Happy Birthday, Mr. Riley

Although I never knew you
I would like to stop and say,
I think of you quite fondly
And remember your birthday.

I've heard it said
This was your very favorite time of year,
The sight of frost on punkins'
Was to you a sight most dear.

To see the bees a-buzzin'
Round the apples on the ground,
Reminds me some of you
As I enjoy their hummin' sound.

I like to just imagine you
A-sittin' by your fire,
With pen in hand and sippin'
On a cup of apple cider.

As I remember now your birthday
At this time of year,
I'd like to tell you 'thank you'
For your poems, and their cheer.

They make this time of year more special
Stories told by you,
Describing fall in all its splendor
Coloring its hue.

So, "Happy Birthday, Mr. Riley"
I would like to say,
And, "thanks for sharing all your poems
That I love today."

Martinsville Indiana

Such a grand little town
Tucked away in the hills,
With its quaint little courthouse so neat.
It has history so rich
And it's named, Martinsville,
One can still find some cobblestone streets.

Once a playground for rich
And the movie stars too,
Even Presidents came here to play.
And I'm sure of them
There was made great much to-do,
Although none of them seem to have stayed.

Grand old homes line your streets
That are shaded by trees,
That are certainly centuries old.
And the courthouse
Where couples bowed on bended knee,
Is perfection, a wonderful mold.

With its mineral springs
Bubbling up from the ground,
People came for their sickness to go.
Makes you wonder
If all of their minds were that sound,
'Course 'twas only for those "in the know".

Well now Martinsville
You've really not changed at all,
You are still quite a sight to behold.
Tucked away in your beautiful hills
That enthrall,
There are still probably chunks of pure gold.

Well you're now my home town
And we've built our new home,
All surrounded by beautiful hills.
And from here
We are never again going to roam,
From this quaint little town, Martinsville.

Beyond

Beyond the stars,
Beyond the haze,
Beyond the universe I gaze,
Beyond the blackness far out there,
Beyond where mortal eyes now stare.

Beyond is where I dream about
Beyond is real, I have no doubt.
Beyond is where I long to go,
Beyond is where? I do not know.

Beyond is where my real home lies.
Beyond the stars, beyond the sky,
Beyond is where I'll be some day.
Eternally beyond, I'll stay.

Bein' Sick

'Taint no fun when sickness come,
You'd swear you're gonna die, by gum.
When everthin' ya ate that day,
Just up and gets clean blown away.

I'd swear the poundin' in my head
Is loud enough to wake the dead.
And I'm so cold, with every breath,
I think I'm gonna freeze to death.

But layin' here upon my bed,
I guess I'll not yet join the dead.
But for a while was touch and go,
Ya know I just hate sickness so.

The next time that some little germ
Tries to inside my body worm,
I'll shut my mouth and not give in,
So I won't get that sickness then.

Tripping

A trip is such a little thing
Brought often by not noticing
A curb, or a misguided step,
A dog, or other cherished pet.

And how a trip can make a Queen
Appear as though she's bumbling
When she's observed just stumbling
While strolling down the lane.

But oh, what joy a trip can bring,
Though not to those, it's humbling
While in its grasp it does appear
Their gracefulness has disappeared.

A little trip will still remain
To some, great joy, and others, pain.
I cannot change though try I might
To squelch my glee when you take flight.

One Hundred Two

This poem's meant to honor you.
For now you are one hundred two.
Just like the sky your eyes so blue
Still sparkle like they always do.

Just think, three centuries you have seen,
And all the years there in between,
Your life has cast on us a sheen
Of simple times, and living clean.

Today your birthday, and we say,
"A loud hurrah! Hooray! Hooray!
For your life's shown to us the way
That we should live our lives today.

So on this day we honor you,
And cherish those sweet eyes of blue.
And wish you Happy Birthday too,
For you are now One hundred Two.

Dedicated to Ethel Taylor

My Elizabeth Ann

I don't know the Raggedy Man,
But I do know Elizabeth Ann.
She was born in Lockerbie Square
And all the folks really liked her 'round there.

Now I don't know if Elizabeth Ann
Was a good friend of the Raggedy man,
Or if their paths crossed there on Lockerbie Street
Where Elizabeth Ann ran 'round in bare feet.

When Elizabeth Ann and her pals in the square
Would dig in the dirt on the lot that's all bare,
For treasure she'd dig and in hopes that she'd find
A coin in the dirt that would glitter and shine.

I'll bet you those times that the Raggedy Man
Wished that he knew my Elizabeth Ann.

Now the years that she spent in the Square were just eight,
But Elizabeth Ann thinks those years were just great.
Down the cobblestone streets she would run there and play
With the cool autumn breeze in her hair all the way.

Yeah, I'll bet you for sure that the Raggedy Man
Wished that he knew my Elizabeth Ann.

Though Elizabeth Ann moved from Lockerbie Square
Leaving behind all the friends she'd made there,
She still likes to return and in hopes that she'll meet
That old Raggedy Man there on Lockerbie Street.

Yeah, I'll bet you for sure that the Raggedy Man
Wished that he knew my Elizabeth Ann.

Dedicated to Elizabeth Ann Robinson

The Circus, Inside Out

The lightning cracked, the thunder rolled,
Yet we were undeterred
For to the circus we must go,
Along with this vast herd.

Though buffeted by sheets of rain
The cold wind in our face,
Our circus tickets we must buy,
Or others take our place.

When finally we reached the door,
A sight to then behold.
As far as we could see were people, huddled,
Young and old.

The line was long, but by and by,
Were tickets in my hand.
And when we saw three rings down there,
'Twas quite a sight most grand.

Right then the tigers in one ring
Were jumping fiery hoops,
But as we tried to find a seat,
All we could say was OOPS.

While stumbling 'oer the people there,
We finally found a seat.
The circus lay before us now,
Right there beneath our feet.

Mark Crouch

We watched the clowns, the dog show,
And the girls on the trapeze
The human cannonball shot out,
And everyone was pleased.

The elephants came out,
And all seemed to perform quite well.
That is except for one,
And what he did I just can't tell.

Now we've been to the circus.
Of that there can be no doubt.
Which one most entertaining, though,
Was it inside or out?

Old City Hall

They say Old City Hall has spooks that haunt the place,
But as of yet I haven't seen a scary face.

Downstairs where the old jail was, is 'spose to be,
Where most ghosts have been seen, or least what they told me.

I wonder if it's true these stories that I hear,
Or do they just embellish them from year to year?.

Why do ghost stories seem to just intrigue us so?
The answer to that question, well, I just don't know.

So, if you're at Old City Hall just having lunch,
Remember then this story as you start to munch.

You may be entertaining someone you don't know,
The likes of which just might make all your blood run cold!

Bay City, Michigan

A Land So Fair

If er'er there were a time or place
Where pain might somehow be erased,
I'd run there swiftly if I could
To that fair land where all is good.

A land in which there are no tears,
A perfect place devoid of fear.
Where darkness, gloom are overthrown,
And all disease is there disowned.

Where might a place as this exist?
Where purest joy it doth consist?
Where all are equal, everyone,
And mercy reigns, as does the Son.

Of course 'tis Heaven I describe,
Where those who love God will reside.
If while on earth their hearts did give
To Jesus, there they too shall live.

A Favorite Rhyme

Of all the poets who have lived,
And all the stories that they give.
To those of us who love to hear,
I wonder which one is most dear.

I can't begin to name them
Such a task is far too hard.
At just the thought of trying to
My mind becomes like lard.

I'll probably never live to see
The day they'll all be read to me,
So how am I supposed to know
The ones to keep or just let go?

And when a poem brings one peace
It may be deemed a masterpiece,
And such a one has touched my soul
Its name was simply called The Rose.

So though I cannot seem to write
Like those of old, though try I might,
I shall not, no, I dare not quit
Describing life through my own wit.

For maybe just like a machine
Not yet invented, such a theme
Might come into a mind like mine
And thus become a favorite rhyme.

Where Ferns Grow

Below the wind just out of reach,
There lies a place I now beseech.
Might bid me entrance there to dwell,
'Amongst the ferns to rest a spell.

To listen to the languid flow
Of water o'er the rocks below.
While up above the winds rage on
Just like the life out there beyond.

Down here the dogwoods in full bloom
Unleash their fragrance, sweet perfume.
Unmindful of the storm above,
I listen to the cooing dove.

There's scant a breeze to toss the ferns,
Here where they live all noise is spurned.
Their secret's safe and I'll not give
Directions to where these ferns live.

Our Birthdays

It's once again the time
To think of birthdays that we've had.
And since mine is so near to yours,
I think about you, Dad.

Of all the times we've shared a cake,
Of laughter that was ours to make,
While birthdays we did celebrate,
Together through the years.

It's not so much to count the years,
But just to think of times most dear,
While sharing birthdays that were near,
Both in December of the year.

So though we are apart this year
I'll still remember when
We'd blow out all the candles
On the cake, or try again.

Now though we're probably neither one
Just thrilled about our age,
Remember all our good times
As we turn another page.

HAPPY BIRTHDAY

Exposing Easter Myths

Would somebody please tell me
Where the Easter Bunny's from?
And who it is that brought about
This yarn that has been spun?

'Cause what this bunny has to do
With Easter, I don't know.
And what's the cause for such
A silly myth like that to grow?

And then there is the
Easter egg, again I'm really stumped
But when the kids go hunting for them,
Man, do they get pumped!

So what do eggs and bunnies
Have in common I can't say.
And who associated them with
Easter anyway?

I see no harm in bunnies, or
In egg hunts, either one.
But Easter clearly is about
God's one and only Son.

Yes, Jesus came and died for us,
And then He rose again.
We celebrate at Easter now
The risen Son of Man

So go ahead and hunt for eggs
And look for bunnies too.
Just don't forget that Jesus
Died and rose again for you.

Summer's 'Round The Corner

These cool days won't be lasting long
With all the birds in raucous song.
Soon 'round this lake will be a throng,
'Cause Summer's 'round the corner.

For now, no bugs on me descend
While in my garden now I tend.
No sweating while my house I mend
But Summer's 'round the corner.

I love the feel of late spring days,
Thick dew amidst the morning haze,
Cool breezes I feel as I gaze,
But Summer's 'round the corner.

I soak up gladly spring-like sun
To me this is the best of fun,
And I'll not stop till Spring is done
'Cause Summer's 'round the corner.

I hate to see these spring days go
But go they will, for that I know,
I'll try hard not to miss them so
'Cause Summer's 'round the corner.

Rhymes For You

If I knew you and you knew me
What might there be to use?
Perhaps a certain favorite phrase
To make a rhyme for you.

Or maybe I could tell about
Your eyes so crystal blue.
Then I could write your poem
And create a rhyme for you.

Just maybe there's a flower
And you love that flower's hue.
Then I could tell its story
And create a rhyme for you.

Or how 'bout that lost love you had
And thought would stick like glue?
Would I dare tell that story
And create a rhyme for you?

Perhaps a note to someone
With a gift that shines so new,
I'd tuck it neatly in a card
And there, a rhyme for you.

No matter the occasion
If I just only knew.
Then I would do my best
To just create a rhyme for you.

Hatchet Man's Bridge

The story goes about a lad and lass
One fateful night.
And how their blissful love
Was then turned into fateful fright.

Now though the lad was trying
From his lass a love to cull,
All that he ended up with
Was a hatchet in his skull.

Though someone must have watched them
Lurking high up on the ridge,
The hatchet caught him cleanly
In the forehead, on the bridge.

That lass was left there screaming
And has never to this day
Expressed a word of what took place
To everyone's dismay.

Though some have speculated
That it was the lass' fault
She uttered 'nar a word
Her lips now sealed there in her vault.

Perhaps the answer lies
Within the house up on the ridge.
But no one dares go near the place,
Called Hatchet Man's Bridge.

146

Noble

I had a dog named Noble once
A long long time ago,
And he, my best friend ever
Always wanted just to go.

Alongside me no matter
Where the destination lay,
And just be there close by my side
To deal with come what may.

No finer dog could e'er be found
Or will be e'er again,
This noble dog, I think of still,
Remains my truest friend.

He was a German Shepherd
And his fur a solid white,
He seemed to glisten when the moon
Would shine on him at night.

If he was ever sick
He never let his feelings show,
For in a moment's notice
He'd be ready then to go.

His big brown eyes would smile at me
As if he'd like to say,
"Come on. Let's go out for a walk
And spend the live long day."

The last thing I remember
As I laid him in the ground,
The sound a breaking heart can make
While left there just to pound.

My hope is that I'll see him one day,
Waiting there for me.
Where through the fields in heaven,
We will romp eternally.

Dedicated to my Faithful Dog Noble

Her Front Porch Home

O little wren, was no spot left
In all the woods for you?
No place to build your little nest
For such small eggs, but two?

Why here on my front porch
Amidst the flower pot you chose
To weave your tiny nest,
Perhaps for me, might I suppose?

I must admit,
The landscape that you've chosen for your nest
Around our little cottage home
I truly like the best.

So why then if you chose my place
And in me put your trust
You keep yourself at such a distance
And put up a fuss?

For you must know by now
That I am not your enemy.
And if I could I'd gladly
Quickly to your needs now see.

O little wren might there still be
A safer place to dwell?
Of course though you're in God's hands
Only time alone will tell.

149

If, as I water gingerly
The flowers around your home,
I one day will see little wrens
To from your nest go roam.

Summertime

It doesn't seem it's been a year
Since Father's Day was here.
What better time to come up with a rhyme
About you, Dad, And what you mean to me
Year after year?
And write it to you in the summertime.

It's summer when the things we did together
Seem most clear.
Like mowing our big yard time after time.
And after washing off the car
You'd throw it in low gear,
Then stop to get some ice cream for a dime.

When I think of vacations with you,
Memories are most dear.
The ones in motel pools are most sublime.
I hope when you think back,
These memories bring to you some cheer,
'Cause I had such a wonderfully good time.

So as I pause a moment
To reflect upon the years,
And write them down for you here in this rhyme
I'd like to say "I Love You".
And to me you are So Dear,
As fondly we remember Summertime.

Happy Father's Day!

Basements

They're things that live in basements
That never show their face.
I know 'cause they've been after me,
And caused my heart to race.

Now my best best guess is that they're snakes,
The thought of them still gives shakes.
The way they chased me up those stairs
Would really give me quite a scare.

They never seemed to bother me
While playing all alone,
But if I tried to go upstairs
They'd scare me to the bone.

It seems the last few stairs
Is when they'd all come rushing out.
But running for my life
I wouldn't dare to turn about.

Then when I'd finally reach the top
And slam the little door,
I'd swear I heard the snakes
As they went crashing to the floor.

I still believe there're things that live in basements,
Just like mine.
And watch those last few stairs
Or you can bet, on you they'll dine.

Grey Days

Like a lovely blanket
That's been neatly draped around
This melancholy grey day
That slipped in without a sound.

The clouds and fog envelop me
And I will now embrace
The gently falling raindrops
As they now caress my face.

A gloomy day to some, but not to me,
I like the sight
Of clouds and fog, the mixture of them
Blended in just right.

And though it seems the sun
Might not appear again at all,
I love the drapery of the clouds
When from the sky they fall.

Now though we all like days
When we can frolic in the sun,
It's nice to have a lovely, foggy, grey day,
Like this one.

Audley Quear

I heard on the news
Of a man, Audley Quear,
And how all the folks
Really liked him round here.

There were some on that farm
Thought he'd just disappeared,
Which seemed sort of strange
For the man, Audley Quear.

As the farmers were frantically
Searching about,
It was then they discovered
The corn had spilled out.

They found to their horror
He'd been covered up there,
So he came to his end
In the corn, Audley Quear.

My Lazy Daze of Summer

My lazy daze of summer
Watchin' as a bumblebee,
Just makes his way around from flower to flower,
Has got me in a trance
And from my porch I see,
No better way to wile away the hours.

The sun is blazing brightly
Not a cloud is in the sky,
And in the breeze the flags just gently wave.
I rock back in my chair
And release a gentle sigh,
For in my mind this perfect day I'll save.

The flowers around the porch
Are spectacular to view,
The pinks and purples are the perfect shade.
The brilliant sun illuminates
Their iridescent hue,
For such a day as this they're tailor-made.

As from my porch I'm caught up
In a daze across the bay,
To watch the gentle breeze push sailboats 'round.
I'll take this quiet moment
Just to marvel at the day,
As I proceed to soak up every sound.

I love to watch the children
Chasing seagulls on the beach,
As they have probably done for centuries now.
I'm sure one day these memories
I will quietly beseech,
And in my mind I'll cling to them somehow.

These lazy days of summer
Won't be 'round much longer now,
Before too long cold winter winds will blow.
But maybe to this front porch
I'll return again somehow,
And bring a summer lazy daze, in tow.

The Call

The call came late that fateful night
Its ringing loud indeed.
I felt no urge to answer it
Just anger, I concede.

So sure that it would stop
If I would just allow it time.
The ringing, though, persisted
'Till I thought I'd lose my mind.

Why must this caller be persistent?
Just leave me alone.
I have no need of anyone
Secure here in my home.

Why must I now be bothered?
It's too late for such a call
To answer it at this late hour
I feel no need at all.

Just then the call grew louder.
Was it real or in my head?
I felt that I must answer it
Or I might soon be dead.

Who could this caller be
For now there's knocking at the door?
Or is this just my heart
That I hear pounding all the more?

Now I must know this caller
Quickly please, identify.
With that I then went to the door
And threw it open wide.

And there the caller, Jesus Christ,
Was waiting just for me.
To give my life to Him,
And with Him, live eternally.

The Town Called Rensselear

I've heard tell there's no finer place
Than little Rensselear
In all of Indiana
Or the Land we love so dear.

Appears though from the highway
It's just another little place
To stop and fill your tank
Or maybe even stuff your face.

What was it Mr. Riley
Seemed to love about it here?
What captured his attention
Here in little Rensselear?

I'll bet he loved the quiet
And the peaceful atmosphere.
That's one thing that they have for sure
In little Rensselear.

So as I go now down the road
And watch it disappear,
I'll think about it different now
This town called Rensselear.

The Crawdad Hole

I've come back for a visit
Back to the crawdad hole,
Where olden days just linger endlessly
In search of the old crawdad
Who meanders kinda' slow,
And makes his way 'round this creek lazily.

The ferns that grow so thickly
As they have throughout the years,
Continue in abundance all around.
Seems nothing can disturb
The tranquil presence that is here,
I'll bet the old crawdad's yet to be found.

Although my feet more wrinkled
As I splash them in the creek,
The water doesn't seem to mind at all.
Who says that olden days are gone
And for them many seek,
When right here I still hear their ancient call?

There still are fallen logs and rocks
That under I now peer,
As once I did when hair was thickly grown
Upon my little boyhood head.
When days were filled with cheer,
It's days like that I never will disown.

161

So as I go in search
Of the elusive old crawdad,
That great big old granddaddy of 'em all,
I think quite fondly of the days
And not the least bit sad
Of crawdad hunting when I was quite small.

Lord willing I'll return again
To the old crawdad hole,
And feel cool water tickling my feet,
'Cause this clear water clearly
Is refreshing to my soul,
And maybe you know who right here I'll meet.

Daddy's Girl

What happened to your little legs
Your little cheeks and eyes?
Your tiny toes and fingers
And your tiny little thighs?

Those little lips that formed a perfect circle
Like an O,
And tiny feet that carried you
When I just watched you go?

What happened to the little girl
That sat up in my lap?
And sometimes fell asleep
And then we'd both just take a nap.

Oh Jessica, I hope you know
You're still my little girl
And I'd love to protect you
From the evil of this world.

But you're all grown up now
And out there driving in your car.
I hope you know you'll always be
My tiny Texas Star.

I'd like to say I'm proud of you
And always will be too.
No matter what may happen
I will stick with you like glue.

163

So, thinking back and missing
All your tiny little curls,
I want to tell you plainly
You are still your Daddy's girl.
I Love You, Daddy

My Squeaky Old Chair

I have just noticed
A squeak in my chair.
I'm sure it has been there
Though I did not hear.

But now that I've noticed
The squeaks in my chair.
I've started to notice
The squeaks everywhere.

Squeaks in the door,
Squeaks in the floor,
Squeaks I've not noticed here
Ever before.

Just why all these squeaks
Have begun to appear
Why now they are brought
To my listening ear
Is more than my mind
Can begin to conceive
I think I hear squeaking now under the eve.

The whole world is squeaking
Real loud if you'll hear,
I bet you will notice it
Just give an ear.

The Candy Man

He comes in with his suitcase
Laden with his tasty treats.
To once again bring all of us
A myriad of sweets.

Invisible to all it seems
Or least that's how it feels,
He goes about his work
And seems content with what life deals.

The candy man whom no one
Ever seems to really know,
We only see him now and then
And watch him come and go.

Just why he caught my eye today
I'm really not quite sure,
Perhaps the way he glanced at me
His countenance demure.

I wonder if he'd like to know
Who frequents his machine,
That some of his best customers
Are miserable and mean!

It's just too bad his candy
Doesn't bring smiles to this place,
The way I've seen it brighten up
A child's little face.

I hope he knows that some
Appreciate his coming 'round
And sometimes just like children
Off to his machine we bound.

The Masterpiece Of Life

I'd like one day to paint a masterpiece
With simple words,
Describing life in such a way
As no-one's ever heard.

To bring to life the wind
That one can witness in the trees,
With words describe contentment
Of a soothing ocean breeze.

How can one tell of quiet calm
In forests thick with pine?
What words might I now call upon
To share these thoughts of mine?

Such force I see as thunderstorms
Explode upon the land,
No words convey my feelings
Though I try as best I can.

With such beauty comes a new day
That I struggle once again.
How can I paint such splendor
When all I have is my pen?

For this day is so stunning
Deep blue sky, and trees so green.
Such vibrant colors cannot be conveyed
But only seen.

Mere words escape me
Trying to describe a child's smile
The twinkle in their eyes,
One could get lost in for a while.

With pen in hand and simple words,
I feel I'm overcome.
To write this masterpiece of life
Just simply can't be done.

The Town of Assiut

Though I have never seen where I was born,
I've heard it told
That there've been people who died there
Whose faces were pure gold.

Now I can't help but wonder
How the village of my birth,
Might have produced this gold,
And all the millions that it's worth.

But that to me is not the reason
That I now reflect.
Is this a land of mystery?
I'm sure that some suspect.

But I just wonder 'bout the town,
Its name is Assiut
Deep in the heart of Egypt
There along the Nile route.

Might it have been the gateway
To the stories that were told
About the Pharoah's faces
That were laden so with gold?

But here I simply wonder
'Bout the place where I was born.
And what then was the weather?
Was it late at night or morn?

I know it was December
Did the day dawn cold or hot?
Does anyone remember,
Or have all simply forgot?

Now none of this important
And it matters not to me.
Yet I can't help but wonder
'Bout this town I've yet to see.

I'm sure that many people
Never saw their place of birth.
And there's nothing about it
That might give me sense of worth.

I guess it's nothing more
Than simple curiosity
Perhaps one day Ill go to Egypt,
Just so I can see

This place where I was born.
So then that question won't be moot.
I finally will see for myself,
This town of Assiut.

The School Bus

My boy got on the bus today,
Just like I used to do.
That big old yellow school bus
That carries him to school.

I rode the bus like he does
When I was in sixth grade.
And on it I had lots of fun
With all the friends I'd made.

They weren't as strict as they are now.
No school bus rules we had.
We never got in trouble,
'Less of course we were real bad.

We'd holler out the window all the time
At passers by.
And every now and then we'd cause
A girl or two, to cry.

We'd switch from seat to seat,
And never really were content
To just sit still until our driver's patience
Was just spent.

But now they give them certain seats,
Assigned, the word they use.
If that was me, the word I'd use
Would probably be refuse.

And these days if he even waves to me,
His dear ole' dad,
He'll probably get in trouble.
Now I think that's pretty sad.

'Cause I think riding on the school bus
Should be lots of fun.
For Lord knows when you get to school
All of your fun is done.

Oreo

Why can't every puppy dog
Be like Oreo?
She's never sick or lazy,
Which just makes you love her so.

She's always quick to flash a smile
That brightens up your day,
And then she shyly bats her eyes
As though she'd like to say,

"I'm just so happy to be here
Part of your family,
I'll not forget the day you showed
Such kindness unto me."

So now I'm truly thankful
That we snatched her from the road.
And took her in to be our friend,
Our dog, named Oreo.

Belated Mother's Day

Belated greeting cards
Are not the kind I like to send.
All the more on Mother's Day
I now must make amends.

I couldn't leave it up to someone else
To write the rhyme,
To tell you Happy Mother's Day
It's up to me this time.

Although it could be said
That I might have a good excuse
To carry on with words like that
I simply see no use.

So now I'd like to tell you
Just how special that you are.
And try to put it into words
On yet another card.

I'm really grateful just to have you
As my "Mother Dear",
I think right now of all the joy
You bring me, year by year.

And that is what I'd like to wish you
On this Mother's Day,
That Joy in great abundance
Would most surely come your way.

The Jaws of Death

The day began with splendor
As the players took their place.
Determination firmly set
Upon each stoic face.

Their daily need for battle
By necessity it seems,
Proceeds without emotion
Though their eyes appear to gleam.

The prize is guarded fiercely
By The faithful sentinel.
And by day's end who'll be the victor?
Only time will tell.

The enemy, though shrewd
Is driven by the flaw of greed.
Insatiable desire they have
For gleaming golden seed.

Their daily ritual begins
Advancing stealthily,
From limb to limb they make their way
Unto the feeder tree.

The enemy arrives on cue
These brazen, taunting squirrels,
To do their best to render chaos
Into this dog's world.

Then suddenly the faithful guard
Goes charging into war,
Which causes all the enemy
To from this tree now soar.

The nearby branches usually
Provide a safe escape,
Though looming is a span of space
That this day seemed to gape.

For one among the enemy
Seemed in the hands of fate.
Just why he missed remains a mystery
For this poor mate.

But missed he did, perhaps the branch gave way.
How's one to know?
What caused this poor unlikely squirrel
To land square in death's throw?

So now what all along was game
Then took a sudden turn,
The ground around this fateful slip
Began a wretched churn.

The loyal guard, this dog
Was now faced with a sullen test.
Unhappily, this game had ended
In the Jaws of Death.

A MIGHTY VOICE
"My Tribute To My Uncle Scotty"

Heaven's choir has gained a mighty voice today,
For now my Uncle Scotty's there to lead the way.

I'm sure his voice is booming throughout heaven now,
'Cause I don't know of anyone that sang that loud.

He always sang with gusto and was right on key,
I don't know if he knew how that inspired me.

His singing was just like the way he lived his life,
With great enthusiasm, little time for strife.

I'll miss my Uncle Scotty, but I'll hope one day,
To hear him sing in Heaven's choir his same old way.

Dedicated to my Uncle Scotty

Eternal Breath

God gave mankind eternal Life,
The breath of life He gave.
And then He sent His only Son,
Our wretched souls to save.

For when he gave us life,
The only kind of Life He knew,
Was Life like His, eternal Life,
And from it mankind grew.

'Twas Jesus said, "Eternal Life
Is this: For you to know
The only true God and His Son,
Whom He sent here below."

So now the only way to live
Our lives eternally,
Is something that's so simple
That a child can even see.

We gain this life eternal
Through believing in God's Son.
For Jesus is the only way,
There is no other one.

So one place or the other
You must spend eternity.
Will it be hell or heaven?
It's now up to you and me.

Reflections

The time has come to once again
Reflect upon the day,
And all the mysteries of life
That kindly came my way.

I cannot comprehend them all,
Some pleasant, others pain,
Yet everyday I live this life
There's something I must gain.

Though disappointments come and go
Like fireflies at night,
Then unexpected treasures come
Like shooting stars so bright.

This day taken for granted
By so many that I meet,
As though it's ours to fit somehow
Into our plans so neat.

This mystery called life
That no one truly understands,
I feel is quickly slipping
Just like jello, through our hands.

To those who know Him, one day, God
Will take time to explain
His mystery that we call life,
Where there will be no pain.

So until then I'll try my best
To thank Him for each day.
And do my best to please Him
And to live this life His way.

Discourse

When people want embellishment
Well, clearly I have not been sent
To on them such a thing bestow,
In spite of being "in the know".

I find it tiresome at best
To satisfy their earthly quest
For details of what others do,
And on them cast appalling hue.

For one might first of all require
Some interest in their life, so dire.
So from that I'm eliminated
From thoughts now, or some belated.

So sorry, I can't comment, then,
On other's lives, their raucous din,
And please afford me exit now
To bow out gracefully, somehow.

All In Fun

I suppose I could embark
And tirelessly strive to cease
From working long into the night,
Creating yet another piece.

For what gain would there be in that?
As yet another verse comes forth,
Wherewith to entertain or soothe,
Or try my best to prove my worth.

'Tis futile words that I could give,
My thoughts, no consequence to you,
But out they come I can't refrain,
Or squelch their iridescent hue.

Might I have but one more verse,
With which to hearken soul and wit,
And thus present myself to you,
As simply just a one act skit?

The Drought

A lonesome sight, the creek bed,
All dried up and dusty now,
This drought has squelched its melody.
There sits a rusty plow.

The fields which should be flourishing
With corn and beans and hay
Have yet to feel the rain pour down
Through all the month of May.

No splashing in the swimming hole,
Here in the month of June.
The gleeful cries are stifled
By a hot and dusty tune.

What corn there is stands wilting
As July begins its march
Through dusty farms, as farmers pray
To see the rainbow's arch.

The smell of rain so sweet
Seems all forgotten in the drought.
All eyes toward heaven
Long for God to open up the spout.

Just when it seems that He's forgot,
The rain comes pouring down
To cover all the earth it seems,
A flowing, sparkling gown.

Then once again new life springs forth,
And water starts to flow,
This drought is all forgotten
As the earth begins to glow.

The Promise

I've seen a rainbow once or twice
But not like this one here
Thought I was seeing double
While to heaven I did peer.

But sure enough a perfect double rainbow
In the sky,
I almost didn't look right then
But something caught my eye.

It followed such a storm
That it was kind of nice to see,
The sign that God put in the sky
As if to remind me.

The storms of life will come and go
And some may be quite rough,
But if I trust Him, only God
Knows when to say "Enough".

Don't know if I will ever
Get to see another sign
Just like that double rainbow,
That I'll take from God as mine.

Sittin' Round

I got to go to work today
But that's O.K. with me,
'Cause I've had just about enough
Of sittin' round, you see.

A feller 'n only take so much
Of sittin' 'round the house,
A 'quarlin with his neighbors
Maybe even with his spouse.

Porch sittin's good
But only if it's not too long a spell,
How long that is, well I'd say
That it's kinda' hard to tell.

It takes a couple days
To see that most things stay the same,
But after that you start to wonder
If you'll go insane.

So off to work I guess I'll go
Back to the "daily grind",
And ain't it funny
That I just don't really seem to mind?

I'm sure it won't be long, though
Till I'm longing for that place,
A'sittin' on the front porch
In that old familiar space.

Mark Crouch

This Great Lake

The afternoon pristine,
The air all fresh and clean,
The view from this front porch cannot be beat.
As on the lake I gaze,
All gone the summer haze,
And with it went the stifling summer heat.

Lake Michigan today,
That lies beyond the bay,
Looks like a jewel that sparkles in the sun.
As sailboats pass by,
So pleasing to the eye,
I wish this day had only just begun.

I think the perfect view,
Of this great lake's rich hue,
Is captured best by seagulls as they fly.
And I would like to be,
One of them so I'd see,
If only for a day from a bird's eye.

The breeze that's up today,
Across this little bay,
By this great lake that I now gaze upon,
Is fresh as one could please,
Just like an ocean breeze,
I'd like this day to just go on and on.

The trolley passed just now,
And I believe somehow,
I've been transplanted somewhere back in time.
Or might I just be lost,
And what then is the cost,
To find my way back to my little rhyme.

So as the boats come in,
My thoughts return again
To this great lake and all who hug its shores.
And though I have to go,
This lake must surely know
I'll not forget this day, forever more.

Mark Crouch

Boss Of The Bayou

Down in the land of Spanish moss
That hangs upon the trees,
Like giant grass skirts gently swaying
In the summer breeze.

I came upon a quiet bayou
Languidly it lay.
Beside the road I traveled
On this hot and sultry day.

Across it lay an old bridge
Boarded up and long forgot,
Whose shade trees offered refuge
From the days that grow so hot.

'Twas from this vantage point
I chose to spend the afternoon
In hopes I'd spy an alligator,
Possibly a loon.

I wasn't disappointed
For quite shortly there arose
An alligator from the murky depths
In slight repose.

Although it was quite small
I was elated just to see
This little alligator
Swimming right up close to me.

I watched it as it moved about
So stealthily it seemed
As though it played a role
In my Louisiana dream.

So on this lazy afternoon
Amidst the Spanish moss,
I caught a glimpse of what some say
Is simply Bayou Boss.

The Unknown Poet

I can't nor would I dare compete
With poets that are known,
For using words just like a brush
Their paintings thence are shown.

Might I describe a rose
As though a soul resides within,
And try therefore to bring to life
A flower with my pen?

Why should I even try to tell
What lives inside my mind?
I dare say it's been said before
With words more grand than mine.

I might not see a honeybee
The way a master would.
To cause its sound to spring to life
For you, I doubt I could.

But even with these feelings
I'm not daunted, but compelled
To bring to life the stories
Only I alone can tell.

Counting Your Blessings

I've been reminded recently
Of things I cannot do.
So those are now the very things
I'll strive to here think through.

I cannot run, I cannot play.
The pain is too intense.
But just to sit and dwell on this,
To me, makes no good sense.

I'd rather ponder all the many things
I can do now.
Perhaps there're many things I will
Enjoy the more, somehow.

I still can sit and listen
To the babbling of the brook,
And watch the bumblebees enjoy
The nectar that they took

From flowers that smell so sweetly
That I'm able to enjoy,
While listening to the birds in song
Whose raptures I employ.

To coax me thus into a state
Where troubles melt away,
And give to me the strength I need
For yet another day.

It's true that troubles come our way
To those of us on earth.
My thought is how we handle them
Distinguishes our worth.

So I'll now dwell on things I can do
Rather than I can't.
When tempted to feel sorry for myself,
I'll say I shan't.

Moonshine

I growed up in Missoura
Down a'mungst the Ozark hills.
You know, down in the hollers
Where they fire up the stills.

Now you might think that moonshine,
Why, it ain't much made no more.
You ain't been to Missoura
Just come look out my back door.

You see the smoke a-risin' up
Down in the holler there?
Just wait a spell and you'll smell moonshine
Waftin' through the air.

See, down here in Missoura
What they call the "show-me" state,
We pass the time just sittin' 'round
A-sippin' moonshine, late.

We still go huntin' coons
Just like we did so long ago.
And I don't guess we'll ever stop
Just takin' life real slow.

We like to run 'round barefoot
Even in two thousand one.
And if that ain't your style, well see,
That don't bother me none.

So if you're in Missoura
Go on out a-mungst the hillls.
And have a sip of moonshine,
Just don't mess with any stills.

The Test

When thinking one day of the purpose of life,
Trying hard not to be too profound,
It occurred to me then that the answer I sought
Might not want to be easily found.

For I know that my purpose can't possibly be
On the earth, to just wander about,
For the time that I have here no matter how long
Is quite limited, and there's no doubt.

Though I love to go out in the woods and observe
How the creatures there live day to day,
I don't think that's the reason that I have been born,
Just to sit there and watch them, no way.

Perhaps like in school, life is just one big test.
If I answer correctly I'll see
Just what's waiting beyond in the life that's to come
That God gladly will give unto me.

So I think that the question to what life's about,
And the answer that I'm searching for
Lies in looking to God everyday that I live,
And not wondering if there is more.

The Old Pinball Machine

I still hear the sound,
The noise that it made
While racking up games,
Drinking pink lemonade.

The thrill that I got,
The money not green,
Fed constantly
To the old pinball machine

It cast such a spell,
This machine that I played.
Till by it a fool,
I had simply been made.

But luck would then change,
And from it I'd win.
Could playing this game
Be some sort of sin?

There're times that I wondered
If it was just mean.
This thing that I loved,
The old pinball machine.

Moods

Alas, the clouds have gathered.
I can't make them go away
No matter what I think or do,
Or to myself I say.

For when this thing that's known as mood
And whether good or bad,
Decides to settle in a while
I might be glad or sad.

I hear it said 'most every day
By someone that I know,
"I'm just not in the mood right now"
For this or that, you know.

So is a mood a real thing
With a mind that's all its own?
Or just one's own behavior
That's controlled by them alone?

Well, if that's true I guess my mood
For writing this has changed.
I'll stop right here. Is that my mood?
Or am I just deranged?

Grand Haven

Grand Haven on Lake Michigan at best,
Can only be described in words as rest.
And in it I am only but a guest,
Along with all the rest.

Its tranquil beaches lie in quaint repose,
The air is sweet and fragrant to the nose.
Be careful on the lake the saying goes,
I will, O goodness knows.

Grand Haven is a harbor here for ships,
And many are the sizes of its slips.
As people on their porches take their sips,
And offer up their quips.

The shopping in this little town is grand,
As I peruse the shops from where I stand.
The food is also not so very bland,
Despite the taste of sand.

Grand Haven is the perfect little place,
The smiles here are abundant on each face.
There's nothing here to make one's face grimace,
The path here to, I'll trace.

Thoughts of Noble

When October goes away,
A certain sadness comes my way.

Like ceaseless rain on window pane,
I'm flooded now with sad refrain.

The trees now bare in winter's stare,
And through the moon's relentless glare.

My tears resume with timeless gloom,
In thoughts of you 'neath winter's plume.

But joy resides now deep inside,
In knowing that not there you hide.

But in a world that's yet to be,
'Tis there that you wait, just for me.

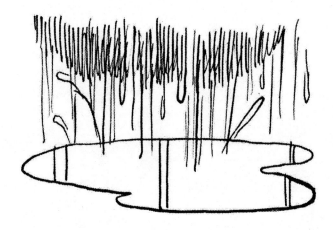

Lovely Rain

I love to wake on Saturday
And hear the sound of rain.
To lie and listen to it pound
Upon my window pane.

To know I needn't hurry
On this day, no need to rush.
Just listen as the rain
Brings to the earth a certain hush.

No bouncing balls, no barking dogs,.
Ceased is activity.
Just why this brings me joy
Is such a mystery to me.

But I'll not bother here
To wonder why or to explain.
For I would much prefer to listen
To this lovely rain.

Sunday At the Beach

What better way to spend the afternoon
As breezes blow,
Then at the beach relaxin' in the sun.
If you've a better way
Well then I'd surely like to know,
This day was tailor made for lots of fun.

The kites are soaring
In the onshore breeze, today that's strong,
As seagulls seem to in the air mark time.
And on the beach is gathered there
A sandy, sweaty throng,
A perfect match for such a Sunday rhyme.

The dunes along the beach
Are laden with a sandy plume,
That seems to stretch forever endlessly.
How long might such a day as this exist?
One can assume,
That night will only come much too quickly.

As ships come into harbor
By the lighthouse on the pier,
A smattering of people shyly wave.
I love the beach on Sunday afternoon
Its atmosphere,
Is what my mind will now forever save.

Back Roads

No sweeter sight could 'er be seen,
No cars in front, nor in-between.
And backwards far as eye can see,
No one here on the road but me.

These back roads that I love to roam,
Could easily be called my home.
Why is there here such great appeal?
I love them, though, I know that's real.

These back roads beckon all the time,
Not just to fill this space in rhyme.
When time is right I'll quickly go
Down paths I fondly call back roads.

To Be

You ever feel it's all been said
There's nothing left to say?
Well, that's the way I feel right now
On this most splendid day.

What can I add with words
That haven't all been said before?
As though I could somehow unlock
A secret, hidden door.

I think there're times in life
When words just simply aren't enough,
To bring to life the feelings that I have,
It's just too tough.

So I've decided on this walk
To simply just exist,
Though thoughts of trying to explain
Continue to persist.

But I shall not give in.
For I'm determined now to see
That as I simply close my mind
Just what it's like to be.

Inanimate

I find it odd, in fact, most queer,
A strange phenomenon I fear,
To let my anger now be sent
At objects called inanimate.

When I get angry at my shoes,
It's always I who tends to lose.
For if in vengeance, them attack,
I find that they might just kick back.

Perhaps a door that shut too soon,
That I might strike, like some buffoon.
While reeling, then, my hand in pain,
I run into the door again.

Up to a window I would go
To let the cool fresh breezes blow.
When it won't budge, I'm tempted then
To hammer it, again, again.

Why is it when a chair I bought,
Between a wall and door gets caught?
I have the urge, and wish I could
Just pound it into firewood.

So why it is, I do not know,
I'm angered by these objects so?
But to these feelings I consent
To smash things called 'inanimate.

Time

The clock is ticking loudly
As it hangs there on the wall,
Though I don't want to hear it
It's resounding down the hall.

I'd like right now for time
To just slow down and take a rest,
For right now is the time
That I am feeling at my best.

This seems to be the time
When time begins to speed ahead,
These times I want to savor
I begin to now feel dread.

So why at times does time move fast
And other times move slow?
Of course it's always constant
This is a fact, I'm sure you know.

There's never time enough it seems
For things you love to do.
But while awaiting some event
Time seems to drag you through.

Some say that time moves faster now
Than it has moved before,
To me this makes no sense at all
Perception, nothing more.

So to a forest I have come
To measure time today.
My findings are that time is measured
In the same old way.

So if you feel the clock
Has somehow gained a stroke or two,
Just walk through some old forest
And let time then speak to you.

An Inner Look

If you might pardon me
And give a moment of your time,
And journey with me down the path
That leads me through this rhyme.

You see, in the beginning
I'm not sure which way to go,
For as I look ahead
I see a fork there in the road.

To me a poem's like my life
I live from day to day,
Just one line at a time
But not real sure I'll find the way.

So at this fork here in my path
I find a question looms,
If I now choose the wrong way
Could it spell for me my doom?

But whether rough or easy
One must always plod ahead,
For life is constant motion
The alternative, you're dead.

So through my eyes you now see
How my poems do begin,
And even at this moment
I'm not sure how it will end.

Like life a poem can be
Just a simple pan-to-mime,
I hope you see my message
As we've journeyed through this rhyme.

Mark Crouch

The Storm

The sound of distant thunder
The hills alive with rain,
The pines bow down beneath the load
As if in constant pain.

The storm in all its fury
Though slow in its approach,
The wind like phantom horses
Strain to pull the heavy coach.

Such fury is unleashed
And havoc reeked there in its wake,
The greedy storm demands from victims
All their lives to take.

Such force of wind
Can only be described here as a gale.
The battering that was to come
Began with loads of hail.

The house that was a home
Then just exploded in the night.
The dreadful storm had left behind,
A sad and tragic sight.

As always, in the aftermath
The sun shone bright next day.
But no one will forget The Storm
That came that night in May.

Down To Earth

I've heard it said, "You're down to earth".
But where else can I be?
Perhaps the Moon, or Mars, or Saturn,
Floating aimlessly.

That saying has perplexed me some
I must admit right here.
I guess there's some among us
Who live in the atmosphere.

They probably come down now and then
When ailments arise,
Perhaps a nasty toothache
From the pain they too will writhe.

So when I meet a person
That they say is down to earth,
I 'spose they are referring somehow
To the person's worth.

I'm glad though that we're equal
When seen through the eyes of God.
And most of us are down to earth
While through this life we trod.

The Old Man

I watched an old man
As he contemplated life pass by.
Was he content to be there,
As he breathed a gentle sigh?

Or was he thinking of his younger days,
Now gone and spent?
And of the years he'd seen gone by,
And what they now had meant?

I watched him smile at children
As they paused to look at him,
And as they wandered on their way
His face would then turn grim.

I watched him as he cast a glance at lovers,
Hand in hand.
And then he'd look away real fast,
As if in reprimand.

With head down for the longest time,
I'd think, 'he's fast asleep'.
As passers-by would stop and look,
He'd utter not a peep.

But then as if responding to some signal,
He'd look up
To smile at yet another child
There romping with his pup.

Then quiet satisfaction
Would spread quickly to his face,
And all around it was as though
Sheer joy encamped the place.

I watched as then the old man
With a twinkle in his eye
Got up and stretched, and toward me sauntered,
And as he then drew nigh

At first I couldn't focus,
But was startled then to see
The old man I'd been contemplating here,
Was simply me.

Sunset

As the sun goes down
Upon this day that's been so fair,
It's then I get a yearn'in
Just to go down with it there.

Down where it takes another's night
And turns it into day,
And if they choose,
It then will take their burdens far away.

With each new day it brings the hope
That someone's waiting for,
And then it's off again
To yet another distant shore.

So, as the sun comes up today
I'll greet it with a grin,
For I know it's been 'round the world,
But now it's back again.

About the Author

From the time of his birth in an Egyptian city 200 miles south of Cairo, Mark Crouch has had an insatiable urge to be outdoors, either exploring the woods nearby, the trees of far-a-way forests, the beaches of oceans or lakes, the animals and birds encountered, or just plain everyday folks met in his journeys.

Having worked in a number of different vocations from sales to management, some of which afforded him the luxury of travel, Crouch was able to observe wildlife and nature often in their isolated beauty.

It was not until in his early '40's that his gift of poetic expression surfaced. The breadth of this expression is displayed in wide variety in his describing his romp with his faithful dog to the beauty of the grandeur of the Alaskan mountains in Alaska. Travel now with him on his nostalgic journey in the world of beauty and awe.

greatlakescable@yahoo.com
Custom poems for any occasion.
Contact for more information.